A Pocket Guide to

HAWAI'I'S BIRDS

Text by H. Douglas Pratt

Photographs by Jack Jeffrey
and H. Douglas Pratt

MUTUAL PUBLISHING

*T*he mid-ocean mountaintops that we call the Hawaiian Islands received their plants and animals as chance arrivals that could survive 2,500-mile ocean journeys from the nearest continents. The Islands' generous rainfall and balmy trade winds provided a benevolent environment for the successful few. From these chance ancestors, an array of species unique to Hawai'i gradually evolved. ■ The Hawaiian Eden included no land mammals, no amphibians, no reptiles or mosquitoes. Here, birds could safely lose the power of flight, which many did. Plants could lose their thorns and chemical defenses. And by interisland colonization, many species could evolve from a single ancestor. ■ This world, which was like no other, began to change about 1,500 years ago with the arrival of humans from islands to the south. About half of Hawai'i's unique birds, including almost all of the flightless ones, became extinct between the coming of the Polynesians and the arrival of Europeans. We know these hapless birds only from their bones. Following Captain Cook's "discovery" of the Islands, Hawaiian birds faced new challenges and many could not cope with the rapid changes. As native birds died out, island people imported replacements from around the world. In this respect, Hawai'i's birds mirror her human population with the first community now reduced to a remnant and outnumbered by recent immigrants. ■ Today, nearly all of the flowers and trees seen in Waikiki are imports that can be seen in any tropical resort, and the birds can be found in cages in any pet store. But, like modern Hawai'i's people, her present-day birds form a beautiful and cosmopolitan community that is unique in its own right. ■ In the following pages you will meet the surviving native birds, as well as their immigrant neighbors. We hope that these photos will pique your curiosity and lead you to visit some of Hawai'i's remaining wild areas. But, even if you visit only Waikiki, this book will help you to appreciate the birds that today inhabit what Mark Twain called "the loveliest fleet of islands that lie anchored in any ocean."

Library of Congress Catalog Card
Number 96-078613
ISBN 1-56647-145-1

First Printing, December 1996
Second Printing, May 1998
Third Printing, April 1999
3 4 5 6 7 8 9

Design by Angela Wu-Ki

Mutual Publishing
1215 Center Street, Suite 210
Honolulu, Hawaii 96816
Ph (808)732-1709
Fax (808)734-4094
Email: mutual@lava.net
URL: http://www.pete.com/mutual

This book contains in pocket-size format
the entire text and photos of Hawai'i's
Beautiful Birds.

Photo Credits: All photos by Jack Jeffrey,
except those indicated by the initials DP,
which are by Douglas Pratt. Paintings are
by Douglas Pratt.

Printed in Taiwan

TABLE OF CONTENTS

■

Representative Honeycreepers

EVOLUTION ON ISLANDS:

The Hawaiian Honeycreepers

■

Palila

*S*cientists believe that among the first birds to colonize the Hawaiian Islands was a rather undistinguished species of finch related to such mainland birds as goldfinches, crossbills, and redpolls. This seed-eating finch founded a dynasty that became the dominant group among Hawaiian forest birds. We know them today as the Hawaiian honeycreepers, because many species feed on nectar, but in fact they exhibit a range of variation unequaled in any continental bird family. Unfortunately, many of the variants are now extinct, but enough survive to provide an exciting picture of the phenomenon scientists call *adaptive radiation*.

'Akepa

'Akikiki

Hawai'i Creeper

Maui 'Alauahio

VARIATION ON A THEME

■ Some of the descendants of the first honeycreeper, such as the **Palila**, adapted for eating seeds of the mamane tree, retain the thick finch bill, but most have it modified in some way to adapt to new plants and new foods. The bill of the **'Akepa** looks superficially finchlike, but has crossed tips (which you can see if you look closely) used to pry apart the scales of leaf buds in the search for insects. The **'Akikiki**, also called Kaua'i Creeper, is an ersatz nuthatch that picks insects from the bark of trees, while the **Hawai'i Creeper** behaves similarly, but likes smaller branches and twigs. The **Maui 'Alauahio**, also called Maui Creeper, uses its simple straight bill much like continental warblers to glean insects from leaves and bark. On Kaua'i, the **'Anianiau** has a similar bill, but its brush-tipped tubular tongue

'Anianiau

'Apapane

adapts it for nectar as well as insects. Other honeycreepers, such as the abundant crimson **'Apapane** and the fancy **'Akohekohe** or Crested Honeycreeper have slightly down-curved bills and sip nectar from the shallow flowers of ohi'a-lehua. The 'akohekohe even returns the favor by distributing pollen with its bushy crest. Other nectar-feeders have strongly curved bills that fit the tubu-lar corollas of many native flowers. They include the spectacular **'I'iwi** and the **Kaua'i 'Amakihi**, which has close relatives on the other islands.

To these varied, but rather con-ventional, birds we can add the rare **Maui Parrotbill**, whose huge bill and powerful neck muscles enable it to crush twigs and wrench off strips of wood and bark in its search for insect larvae. But perhaps the most bizarre of all is the Big Island's 'Akiap-ola'au (next page).

Maui Parrotbill

'I'iwi

'Akohekohe

Kaua'i 'Amakihi

WHATEVER WORKS: THE AMAZING 'AKIAPOLA'AU

■ Woodpeckers are very poor at crossing salt water, and none ever reached Hawai'i. The woodpecker niche was filled, Rube Goldberg fashion, by one of the curve-billed Hawaiian honeycreepers. Holding its thin upper bill out of the way, the **'Akiapola'au**, or 'Aki for short, uses its straight lower bill to peck at the bark (the Hawaiian name means, roughly, "hammerhead"). Then the upper one comes into play to winkle grubs out of the cracks. The bright yellow males have bigger bills and somewhat different feeding sites than the grayer females.

It All Fits the Bill

■ Hawaiian honeycreepers also exhibit *coevolution*, a process in which two or more organisms evolve simultaneously and develop mutually beneficial characteristics. In Hawai'i, many plants from a variety of families have developed curved tubular flowers that may differ strikingly from flowers of their relatives. Such flowers fit the bills of nectar-feeding birds like a glove on a hand and have the pistil placed so it can pick up pollen from the bird's forehead. The **'I'iwi** shown here is feeding in the curved flowers of **Stenogyne**, a native mint. The red **Kokia** flowers are related to hibiscus, but the petals are rolled into a curved tube. **'Ohe naupaka** is a Kaua'i mountain relative of the straight-flowered *Scaevola* bushes common on tropical beaches. In the lobelia family, **Clermontia** has prominent pistils that are an almost perfect fit for the 'I'iwi. Even the **wiliwili** shows much more curvature than one expects in a member of the pea family.

Kokia • DP

Clermontia • DP

'Ohe naupaka • DP

Wiliwili • DP

Left: 'I'iwi

13 ■

MODERN HAWAI'I'S AVIAN MELTING POT

View of Honolulu • DP

Of you confine your Hawai'i vacation to resort areas such as Waikiki, Ka'anapali, or Kona, you are unlikely to see a native honeycreeper. But birds are always around (even sometimes on your breakfast table!) and a little attention to them will broaden your tropical horizons. In this section we will take you on a bird tour of the Hawai'i seen by most visitors, and the only Hawai'i known to a surprisingly large number of residents, most of whom, after all, dwell in cities and towns.

Great Frigatebird • DP

Common Fairy-Terns

Fairy-Tern egg • DP

Young chick • DP

Older chick

A Few Natives

■ Although Hawai'i's urban areas may look like concrete jungles, they still support a few intrepid native birds. Because the ocean is always nearby, seabirds are often a part of Hawai'i's urban landscapes. **Great Frigatebirds** seem to hang effortlessly in the air high above city streets, and sunbathers at Waikiki are familiar with **Brown Boobies** that course back and forth just offshore. Especially interesting is the **Common Fairy-Tern,** a true urban resident. Although it is a seabird that feeds on small fish, this graceful tern needs trees just as much as it needs the ocean. It has the remarkable habit of laying its single egg on a bare branch without any semblance of a nest. When the fuzzy chicks hatch, they remain on the spot to be fed by their parents. The older chick has long claws on webbed feet which enable the youngster to cling to swaying branches even in high winds. Visitors to Kapi'olani Park in Waikiki or the grounds of the Hawai'i State Capitol can observe these delicate fliers, which the Hawaiians called *manu o Ku*, "the bird of peace," or may see the chicks and adults perched in large trees. Of course, one must be careful not to confuse them with the much heavier and less graceful white **feral pigeons**, descendants of European Rock Doves, that are also abundant in the parks.

Also conspicuous in city parks is the **Pacific Golden-Plover**, one of Hawai'i's most familiar birds. Golden plovers, or *kolea* in Hawaiian, nest in Alaska and migrate to Hawai'i for the winter months. Here, they occupy winter feeding territories in open grassy areas. The same bird will often be in the same spot day after day.

When they first arrive in the fall, they are rather drab, with dirty white underparts and brown upperparts flecked with gold, but they begin to grow black feathers on the breast as the season progresses. By spring they sport a very handsome breeding plumage. Males develop more black than females. It's fun to watch your favorite plover undergo the transformation.

Feral Pigeon • DP

Pacific Golden-Plover Fall juvenile

Pacific Golden-Plover molting • DP

Pacific Golden-Plover spring male • DP

■ One of the first birds the mainland visitor to Hawai'i notices is the **Common Myna**. It is common, bold, and conspicuous and hangs around airports and hotels on all the islands. It is not found in Europe or North America, but has been in Hawai'i since the mid-1800's, when it was introduced from India, supposedly to control insect pests. Mynas are entertaining birds with behavior similar to that of the European Starling, a common mainland relative. Like most starlings, mynas gather in noisy roosts at night, often in dense trees, such as mango, that grow near buildings. Parking under a myna roost can provide a rude awakening the next day! Also immediately noticeable are Hawai'i's two common doves. The little **Zebra Dove**, named for the black-and-white stripes on the sides of its breast, is so bold as to have become a pest in open-air restaurants, where they may land right on your plate! Feeding them is not a good idea for obvious reasons of sanitation. These perky doves, native to Australia, are the source of one of the most familiar sounds in Hawai'i today—the *coo-coo-coo-coo* notes with a rhythm like Morse Code. A bit more reserved, though

still quite tame around hotels, is the much larger **Spotted Dove**. These plump, pink-breasted birds pump their heads back and forth and strut about. Like the mynas, they might well be called *kama'aina* birds. (The term refers to non-Hawaiian families who have lived in the islands for generations.) Their ancestral home is southeast Asia.

Visitors to Waikiki will certainly notice the two bulbuls, introduced in the 1960's, probably as escaped cage birds. Because both of them are crested, some people think they are related to cardinals, but they are native to India and belong to a family that has no American representatives. The **Red-whiskered Bulbul** is the smaller of the two, with white underparts and a very spiky crest. The larger and more common **Red-vented Bulbul** is ubiquitous now

Common Myna

Zebra Dove

Spotted Dove

to look a little closer. One of the most common (some say the most abundant bird in Hawai'i now) is a little green-and-yellow bird with a bold ring of white around each eye. It flits about among flowers and leaves in search of insects and nectar. It is the **Japanese White-eye** known as *mejiro* in its native Japan. Despite its size, it has an impressive tinkling song that may wake you at dawn. Be careful not to mistake the white-eye for the **Yellow-fronted Canary**, another small bird with a lot of yellow in its plumage. The canary, a native of southern Africa, has a seed-eating bill and sings a wonderfully melodic song not quite as complex as that of the familiar yellow canary. Yellow-fronted Canaries love the ironwood trees in Kapio'lani Park but have also spread into native forests on the Big Island. They can be seen on the ground, as well as in the treetops.

on O'ahu and can even be found at the tops of the mountains in dense forest. Both bulbuls are potential threats to native forests and agriculture, particularly for growers of guava, papaya, and other soft fruits. Fortunately, bulbuls seem to hate to fly over salt water and will not spread to other islands without human assistance.

The doves, mynas, and bulbuls are hard to miss, but to identify the numerous smaller birds you will have

Another tiny bird likely to be seen on grassy lawns is the **Java Sparrow**, with bold white cheeks and a huge coral-pink bill. Java Sparrows sometimes travel in huge flocks and can be devastating to grain and other crops. Their importation into the U. S. has been prohibited for years, but they were slipped into Hawai'i anyway in the 1960's and are now spreading, unfortunately, like wildfire.

Red-whiskered Bulbul • DP

Red-vented Bulbul • DP

Japanese White-eye • DP

Yellow-fronted Canary

Another *kama'aina* bird is the **House Finch**, a native of North America. Female House Finches are drab, streaky-brown birds, but the males are washed with raspberry-red, yellow, or orange. The Hawaiian population has a much higher percentage of orange and yellow males than do those on the mainland. It is interesting to see how many of the odd-colored males you can find. House Finches are mainly seedeaters, but they are not very picky eaters and have adapted to a wide variety of habitats in the islands. Completing the geographic mix are several brightly colored birds from South America.

Java Sparrow

House Finch

Northern Cardinal male

Northern Cardinal female

CARDINALS AND COUSINS

■ Most Americans are familiar with the **Northern Cardinal**, at least as a sports mascot, but are surprised to see it in Hawai'i. Introduced in the 1930's, cardinals have done very well in the Islands. They are widespread but are never as abundant as house finches or white-eyes. In the Northern Cardinal, males and females differ in color, but in the **Red-crested Cardinal**, an import from Brazil, they are alike. (The brown-headed birds you see are juveniles.) Red-crested Cardinals are common on O'ahu, but are not as widespread on the outer islands as

the Northern Cardinal. On the Big Island, a cousin of the Red-crested called the **Yellow-billed Cardinal**, also from South America, is common and conspicuous in the Kona area. It lacks the crest that distinguishes the other cardinals. Like Zebra Doves, Yellow-billed Cardinals can become very tame around restaurants and may beg for handouts at your table. Kona also is home to another immigrant from South America—the brilliant-yellow **Saffron Finch**. Look for it around the Keahole Airport and in rural areas of Kona and South Kohala.

Red-crested Cardinal

Yellow-billed Cardinal

Saffron Finch

Cattle Egret

Red Junglefowl cock • DP

Red Junglefowl hen • DP

Junglefowl chicks • DP

ALONG RURAL ROADSIDES

■ If you leave the resort areas and drive into Hawai'i's scenic countryside, you are sure to notice birds along the roadside. Some of these will be the same as those you met in more developed areas, but others can be seen only away from town. The graceful white birds with long yellow legs and bills that you see around livestock and following mowing machines are **Cattle Egrets**. These remarkable birds evolved on the plains of Africa, where they followed grazing animals and fed on insects and other small animals stirred up by the herd. In relatively recent times, taking advantage of newly opened forests and the spread of cattle raising, the egrets spread from Africa as far as North and South America and

Australia. Cattle egrets were brought to Hawai'i in the 1950's, ostensibly to control cattle pests, and they have thrived here. Those egrets living near airports, however, can be problematic for aircrafts. Whether they would have ever reached Hawai'i on their own, we will never know.

The idea of introducing birds as a food source is as old as the first Polynesian settlers. They brought with them chickens that were little changed genetically from the wild **Red Junglefowl** of Southeast Asia. These ran wild in the forests of Hawai'i and are still common along roadways today, at least on mongoose-free Kaua'i. The cocks and hens look like small game chickens, but note that their legs are usually dark gray or reddish, rather than the golden yellow of domestic fowl. The biggest difference shows up in the downy young, which are streaked like baby pheasants, rather than yellow like barnyard chicks. With the idea of adding to Hawaiian food resources, Captain Vancouver presented King Kamehameha I with turkeys from North America. The King liberated them on the Big Island and forbade hunting them for several years so they could become established. Today, **Wild Turkeys** are frequently seen on the island's ranch lands.

Other game birds have been introduced in recent times. Particularly noticeable around resort areas are three species of francolin (say FRANC-olin, not fran-COLIN). Probably the one most familiar to casual observers is the **Gray Francolin**, commonly seen on golf courses on Maui and the Big Island. These dusty-brown partridges with orange throats are attracted to irrigated places in the midst of a dry habitat. In the same places, look for the handsome **Black Francolin**, with its white cheeks and chestnut collar. Female black francolins could be mistaken for grays, but they have a patch of chestnut on the back of the neck. Both the gray and the black francolin come from southern Asia. The much larger **Erckel's Francolin** has a wider habitat preference and can even be found on the edge of forest along Koke'e Road on Kaua'i. It is easily identified by its chestnut cap and longitudinally streaked breast. Erckel's Francolins are becoming increasingly scarce in their native range in the highlands of Ethiopia and Eritrea because of forest destruction, but they are thriving in Hawai'i. The **Chukar** is another introduced partridge often noticed by visitors. It inhabits dry, rocky areas in the Middle East and has adapted to similar places in Hawai'i, such as the

Wild Turkey • DP

Gray Francolin • DP

Black Francolin • DP

29 ■

Erckel's Francolin • DP

Chukar

Common Peafowl • DP

Short-eared Owl

barren summit area of Haleakala on Maui. The **Common Peafowl** was brought to the Islands more for ornament than for food. These handsome birds from India are not widespread, but have lived on the ranch lands of South Kohala on the Big Island for well over a century. Before the coming of cattle ranching, open habitats were rare in Hawai'i so it is not surprising that few native birds are found in such places. Two, however, have taken advantage of open fields. On all islands, look for the day-flying **Short-eared Owl**, known locally as the *pueo*. It often soars over woods and fields in the manner of a hawk. Hawai'i's only true hawk is the *'io* or **Hawaiian Hawk**, which is confined to the Big Island, where it hunts over cane fields, lava flows, and even the streets of Hilo, as well as mountain forests.

Hawaiian Hawk

LITTLE BIRDS IN THE GRASS

■ Almost any pet store in the world will feature tiny finches and waxbills. These colorful and interesting pets have been popular for centuries, and many have been released in Hawai'i. In the wild they usually inhabit grassy areas where they feed on grass seeds at various stages of development. They travel about in flocks, with sometimes hundreds of birds. The **Nutmeg Mannikin** from southeast Asia became so numerous in 19th-century Hawai'i that it wiped out early attempts to grow rice in the islands, hence its local name, "ricebird." Mannikins (not to be confused with the manakins of the American tropics) tend to be patterned in brown and black with dark bills, whereas the closely related waxbills, such as the **Orange-cheeked Waxbill** now common in parts of O'ahu and spreading on Mauai, are often brightly colored with red bills that resemble old-fashioned sealing wax. The African **Common Waxbill**, has become so abundant on O'ahu that, at a distance, flocks look like swarms of bees. The **Warbling Silverbill**, a bird of dry African savannahs, fits neither category and has a metallic bill. It has become abundant in savannah-like parts of the Big Island and is spreading to similar habitats on Maui, Moloka'i, and O'ahu.

Nutmeg Mannikin

Orange-cheeked Waxbill • DP

Common Waxbill

Warbling Silverbill

SINGERS IN THE WOODS AND FIELDS

■ Sadly, most native birds had disappeared from the areas where people lived in Hawai'i by the middle of the nineteenth century due to destruction of the habitat. Foreign birds were often introduced to replace vanished native species. Many of these were brought to the Islands more for their beautiful songs than for their plumage. In open, grassy country on the Big Island and Maui, look for sparrow-like birds with white outer tail feathers flying up from the shoulder of the road. These are **Eurasian Skylarks** that came to Hawai'i from England via New Zealand. Although not very colorful, skylarks have a spectacular vocal display. They circle high overhead, often nearly out of sight, pouring forth a ringing cascade of song that seems to fill the air. It is easy to understand the poets' fascination with this drab-colored bird. Similarly, the Japanese have long held the **Japanese Bush-Warbler** in high esteem, although it is not much to look at and is so secretive that few people ever see the author of the haunting whistles that have become one of the characteristic sounds of forests on O'ahu and Maui. The bush-warbler, *uguisu* in Japanese, named in imitation of its song, is now spreading to other islands in Hawai'i. In similar forests you may also hear the loud, vigorous, and varied whistled song of the **Melodious Laughing-thrush**, a prized cage singer in China, where it is called the *hwa-mei*. It is said that these birds were introduced to Hawai'i during the Chinatown fire in Honolulu earlier this century, when many were liberated by their owners to save them from the flames. Whatever the case, they are now common on Kaua'i, Maui, and the Big Island, as well. In the bird markets of Singapore and other southeast Asian cities, the most prized singer of all is the **White-rumped Shama**, a true thrush that is almost as lovely to look at as it is to hear. It was brought to Hawai'i over half a century ago and now fills the forests of O'ahu and Kaua'i with its lush, liquid and gurgling flutelike notes. Also popular with oriental bird keepers is the **Red-billed Leiothrix**, which used to be called the Hill Robin. It has a rolling robin-like song and has, indeed, taken to the hills in Hawai'i. It is now quite common in forests of all types from O'ahu to the Big Island.

Eurasian Skylark

Japanese Bush-Warbler • DP

Melodious Laughing-thrush

White-rumped Shama

Red-billed Leiothrix

Ruddy Turnstone

AVIAN VACATIONERS ON THE SHORE

■ On any drive in Hawai'i one is never far from shorelines, where one can find the only group of native birds that still survive in the lowlands. Sandpipers, plovers, and their relatives nest in the arctic but "vacation" in Hawai'i during the winter months. You have already met the Pacific Golden Plover, which chooses a wide variety of habitats. Other species are more often seen along shores. The **Ruddy Turnstone** (*'akekeke* in Hawaiian) and the **Wandering Tattler** (*'ulili*) are two that are frequently seen. The tattler is named for its ringing call, imitated by singers of the popular Hawaiian song "Ulili e."

The very pale **Sanderling**, whose Hawaiian name *huna kai* means "sea foam," will already be familiar to many visitors. Sanderlings are the little birds that retreat like wind-up toys before the waves on beaches worldwide. Hawai'i's shorebird visitors even include an endangered species, the **Bristle-thighed Curlew**. The curlew nests only in Alaska and, during the winter, scatters over the far-flung islands of the tropical Pacific. They winter regularly in the uninhabited Northwestern Hawaiian Islands, but on the main islands they are mainly spring and fall transients. They prefer open, grassy areas.

Wandering Tattler • DP

Sanderling • DP

Bristle-thighed Curlew • DP

Hanalei National Wildlife Refuge • DP

Endangered Birds
of Endangered Wetlands

■ For the ancient Hawaiians the staff of life was poi, made from taro root. Taro grows in water, so vast areas of the lowlands of Hawai'i were made into ponds somewhat like rice paddies. As a protein source, Hawaiians also farmed saltwater fish in artificial shoreline ponds ringed with lava rock. Both of these activities created ample habitat for a group of native wetland birds. Because shoreline land is much more valuable today for resort development, these habitats are now preserved only in a few refuges, such as **Hanalei National Wildlife Refuge** on Kaua'i. Because the habitat is endangered, so are most of the birds found there, although the birds may seem abundant at a given site. (Keep in mind that only a few such places

exist, so the total population of freshwater birds is small.) Probably the most noticeable one is the **Hawaiian Stilt** because of its rather annoying yipping calls. One smart-aleck dubbed it the "pond poodle!" Actually, stilts are graceful and handsome birds with black-and-white plumage and long, coral-pink legs. Also widespread in the Islands is the ducklike **Hawaiian Coot**. It is not a duck—notice its white chicken-like bill with a big knob on the forehead. A similar, but more colorful, bird is the **Common Moorhen**, with a red bill. Although it belongs to a common worldwide species, the Hawaiian population is endangered. The moorhen is much shier than the coot and can be seen only on O'ahu and Kaua'i. It lurks in shoreline vegetation and only rarely

Hawaiian Stilt

Hawaiian Coot

Common Moorhen   Hawaiian Duck • DP

Black-crowned Night-Heron adult

Black-crowned Night-Heron juvenile • DP

swims in open water like the coot. There is, of course, a true **Hawaiian Duck** that is related to the familiar Mallard, but it survives in genetically pure form only on Kaua'i. Although the drakes and hens can be distinguished, both look more or less like female Mallards. One Hawaiian wetland bird that is not endangered is the **Black-crowned Night-Heron**, the same one that is found almost worldwide. It is Hawai'i's only resident native heron, but you might think that the streaky brown juveniles are a different species. During the last century, when wetlands were more widespread in Hawai'i, the islands were popular with waterfowl hunters, but too few ducks are present now to allow for sport hunting. Nevertheless, a few familiar mainland ducks and geese manage to find their way to the islands each winter. The most common is the **Northern Shoveler** with its distinctive broad bill. The **Northern Pintail** often arrives without its characteristic long central tail feathers, but grows them in by spring. Even the smaller forms of the **Canada Goose** occasionally show up and should not be confused with the native Nene (see next section).

Northern Shoveler • DP

Canada Goose • DP

Northern Pintail • DP

Nene at Kilauea Caldera • DP

Nene

Saga of the Nene, Hawai'i's State Bird

■ One does not expect to find a goose living in nearly barren lava flow regions far from fresh water. But the Hawaiian Goose, or **Nene**, has adapted well to such unexpected habitats. Note the reduced webbing between the toes. It feeds on a variety of fruits of low shrubs that pioneer on lava flows. These include a Hawaiian huckleberry called **'ohelo**, the stiff-branched **pukiawe**, whose dry berries look like pink porcelain, and **kukaenene**, so named because its purple-black berries so often color nene droppings! Because they evolved in the absence of terrestrial predators, the native geese had little fear of man, a characteristic that they still exhibit today. They probably survived into modern times only because they lived in the saddle between

'Ohelo • DP

Pukiawe

Nene • DP

Kukaenene • DP

Mauna Loa and Mauna Kea, an area considered *kapu* (forbidden) and feared by the Hawaiians. Nene were saved from extinction by an active campaign of captive breeding and release of birds into protected areas. Although these efforts have restored them to national park lands on Maui and the Big Island, they still do not have self-sustaining populations on those islands. Part of the reason may be that these habitats are not ideal for their goslings who do not receive proper nutrition from their food. The goslings become weak and are more vulnerable to predators like the **mongoose**, an alien predator introduced a century ago to control canefield rats, but which "controlled" native ground-nesting birds instead. Recently, Nene have been released on mongoose-free Kaua'i and appear to be thriving there. They can be seen easily at Kilauea Point. They usually are found in small groups—probably families. Males and females look alike, but first-year young have less contrasting colors. The dark streaks on the sides of the neck are not the result of pigmentation but actually are deep furrows in the soft feathers. Several mainland geese exhibit this same phenomenon. When Hawai'i became a state, the endearing and tame Nene, which at that time had just been brought back from the brink of extinction, became its State Bird.

Mongoose

Nene with admirers • DP

Nene family

MOUNTAIN FORESTS:

The Natives' Last Hope

███

*W*hy do we not see native songbirds around resort areas? In most parts of the world, even areas that have seen comparable ecological alteration retain at least some of their natural inhabitants. Hawai'i's native forest birds are absent even from seemingly good habitat at low elevation. To see them one has to venture to mountain forests above 3,000 feet. The reasons are insidious and complex, but are now fairly well understood. Hawaiian birds evolved in isolation from most bird diseases. Many of these are spread by mosquitoes so, even though migratory shorebirds and ducks might have carried such things as bird pox and avian malaria, no vectors were present to transfer them to the resident birds. The first mosquitoes came to Hawai'i in the early nineteenth century in the water casks of a ship from Central America. These tropical invaders became established in the lowlands, but did not do well in the cooler upper forests. Once the vector was present, bird diseases ravaged the natives just as European diseases decimated the Hawaiian people. Now, native forest birds cling to existence in their mountain forest refuges, but they are under constant assault.

Left: Alaka'i Wilderness,
Kaua'i • DP

'Apapane with mosquito

'Apapane in 'ohi'a

'I'iwi in 'ohi'a

THE BIG TWO AND THE BIG THREE

■ Unlike mainland rain forests, which may have hundreds of tree species forming the forest canopy, those in Hawai'i are relatively species-poor. Where rainfall is high, as in the upper reaches of Kaua'i, the entire canopy may be of a single kind of tree, the usually red-flowered ohi'a-lehua (ohi'a for short). It is a remarkable performer ecologically, being one of the pioneer plants on lava flows as well as the dominant tree in climax forests. Although rarely straight enough to be an important timber tree, ohi'a's gnarled and twisted trunks and branches define the character of Hawaiian forests. Its brushlike flowers lack petals. Its stamens grow out of a cuplike calyx in which nectar, the main food source for the nectar-feeding honeycreepers, collects. The other important canopy tree in Hawaiian forests is **koa**. The koa's sickle-shaped leaves belie the fact that it is actually an acacia. Unlike ohi'a, koa is an important forestry tree. It usually grows mixed with ohi'a in slightly drier areas and rarely forms a closed canopy itself. These "big two" trees support a trio of honeycreepers, with representatives on all the main islands. The locally abundant **'Apapane** is the honey-creeper most likely to be noticed by the casual observer. They are hard to miss in places like Hawaii Volcanoes National Park. They are easily identi-fied by the bold white feathers under the tail that contrast with their crimson body feathers. Lacking the white under the tail is the scarlet

Hawai'i 'Amakihi

Koa • DP

'I'iwi, with its amazing sickle-shaped bill. It is less common than the 'Apapane, but is still easy to find in certain places on Kaua'i, Maui, and Hawai'i. Any native forest that is high enough will have both of these red birds, as well as one of the three species of 'amakihi. All three have downcurved bills shorter than that of the 'I'iwi and yellow-green plumage with a black "mask" that gives them a slightly evil, squinty look. The **Hawai'i 'Amakihi** is found from Moloka'i to the Big Island, while O'ahu and Kaua'i each have their own distinct species. (See below for the Kaua'i 'Amakihi.) At one time there was a fourth honeycreeper common to all the larger Hawaiian Islands—the **'O'u**, a chunky green bird with a yellow head and a thick

hooked bill. Sadly, the 'O'u is now nearly extinct and was never photographed by serious photographers with good equipment. We can show only a rather grainy shot taken by Pratt on Kaua'i in 1975. Except for the "big three," each of the larger islands has its own collection of distinctive species.

'O'u • DP

THE BIG ISLAND'S RICH RAIN FORESTS

■ Because it is more than twice as large as all the other islands combined and is formed mostly by two of the world's tallest mountains (measured from their base on the sea floor), Hawai'i has a much greater range of habitats and much more mountain forest at sufficient elevation to support native birds than any of the others. These forests harbor the richest surviving native bird community in Hawai'i. It includes members of several other bird families, as well as the "big three" honeycreepers and others unique to the Big Island. The **Hawai'i 'Elepaio** belongs to a group of flycatchers found from Australia to the Pacific islands. It is a friendly and confiding bird, whose namesake whistles are a characteristic sound of most forest types on Hawai'i. Its plumage varies from place to place, depending on rainfall. This individual shows by its rich chestnut plumage that it is from a wet habitat. Another non-honeycreeper is the

Hawai'i 'Elepaio

'Oma'o

Hawaiian Hawk

Juvenile Hawk, light phase

'Oma'o, related to thrushes and solitaires of North America. The bird is hard to see with its dull gray and brown plumage, but its lively song is hard to miss and is unlike that of any other Hawaiian bird. The song is easy to hear around the headquarters of Hawaii Volcanoes National Park, but finding the singer is a real challenge. The 'Oma'o is mainly a fruit eater, shown here eating bright red berries of native pilo. In any mountain forest on Hawai'i one can expect to see the *'io* or **Hawaiian Hawk**, which has two color phases. The dark one is mostly sooty black at all ages, while a lighter phase is brown above and

white below as an adult, but has beautiful honey-colored juvenile plumage. The Big Island's honeycreeper specialties include the incredible **'Akiapola'au**, which you met previously on page 10, and the brilliant orange **'Akepa**, smallest of the honeycreepers. 'Akepas feed mainly among leaves where they search out insects, but they also sometimes sip nectar. The two parts of the 'Akepa's finchlike bill are slightly crossed at the tip to aid in prying open places where insects can hide. The dull-plumaged **Hawai'i Creeper** closely resembles the Hawai'i 'amakihi, but has a straighter bill and behaves

'Akepa

Hawai'i Creeper

'Akiapola'au

more like a nuthatch, searching the bark of trees for insects. This native bird community is preserved in **Hakalau Forest National Wildlife Refuge**, the first such refuge to be established solely for forest birds. Even such protected areas cannot prevent the invasion of alien species such as the ubiquitous **Japanese White-eye**, shown here feeding on flowers of akala, the Hawaiian raspberry. A particularly insidious invader is the **Kalij Pheasant**, native to Himalayan forests and introduced as a game bird. The Kalij has become the vehicle of transport for seeds of a variety of noxious weeds and diseases that are now showing up far from "civilization."

Japanese White-eye

Kalij Pheasant

Hakalau Forest National Wildlife Refuge • DP

MAUI'S SPECIAL FOREST BIRDS

■ Maui also has its own set of specialties, all of which happen to be honeycreepers. For some reason, native solitaires and flycatchers either did not survive on Maui in historic times or never lived there at all. The island's most common endemic is the warbler-like **Maui 'Alauahio** or creeper, whose plumage resembles that of the Hawai'i 'Amakihi, but whose voice and behavior are quite distinct. Note the fairly straight bill on the grayish juvenile shown on the next page (a bright-yellow male is shown on page 8). The 'alauahio can be seen easily at Hosmer Grove in Haleakala National Park, which is also home to the "big three."

Maui's other two specialties have been found there as well, but to see them one usually has to venture far away from the highway. In **Waikamoi Preserve** (visitors are allowed here only by permit), a project of The Nature Conservancy adjacent to the national park, one can find both the spectacular **'Akohekohe**, also called Crested Honeycreeper, and sometimes the peculiar **Maui Parrotbill**. The 'akohekohe behaves somewhat like a giant 'apapane, feeding almost exclusively in ohi'a-lehua blossoms. Its odd gurgling song only enhances its rather bizarre plumage. Despite its superficially very dissimilar bill, the parrotbill's feeding methods are rather like those of the Big Island's 'Akiapola'au. It does not peck, but uses its lower mandible to gouge into fissures in the bark of trees, where it finds its main prey of beetle larvae. It may also crush small, dead twigs in its search and even opens pilo berries to look for grubs. Male Maui Parrotbills are brighter yellow and have bigger bills than females.

Maui ʻAlauahio juvenile

ʻAkohekoke

Maui Parrotbill male

Maui Parrotbill female

Kalalau Valley • DP

A World Apart: The Kaua'i Forest

■ The distance between Kaua'i and O'ahu is the greatest separating any of the main Hawaiian Islands. This physical distance has had its effect on the evolution of Kaua'i's plants and animals. With a few exceptions, the entire community has a character all its own. It truly is a world apart. Although Kaua'i is smaller than Maui and Hawai'i, its mountain forests are much more accessible to the average visitor who can find many of its native birds around the overlooks above **Kalalau Valley**. Among them, the two red birds of the "big three" are what one expects, but in place of a single species of 'amakihi, Kaua'i has two that subdivide that niche. The **Kaua'i 'Amakihi** has a much longer and thicker bill than its relatives elsewhere and is much more of a bark picker. Its companion species is the distinctive yellow **'Anianiau**, one of the smallest honeycreepers, with a straighter bill than 'amakihis and warbler-like habits. Also look for another little green bird sporting a yellow fore-head and rump (visible as it flies away), blue-gray finchlike bill, and black face. This is the **'Akeke'e**, a close relative of the 'Akepa (see page 7). The 'Akeke'e also has crossed mandibles that it uses to wedge apart the scales of ohi'a leaf buds. Unlike its red-orange sister species which has

Kaua'i 'Amakihi

'Anianiau

'Akeke'e

'Akikiki

broader tastes, the 'Akeke'e feeds almost exclusively in ohi'a trees. Much rarer than the three green birds is the bark-picking **'Akikiki**, formerly called Kaua'i Creeper, the most nuthatch-like of the honeycreepers. Shown here is a juvenile with its bold white "spectacles." Adults have more dark feathering in the face. Along with the honeycreepers at Koke'e, look for the bold and friendly **Kaua'i 'Elepaio**. The young birds, which are rusty brown rather than gray on the head, are particularly curious. One Kaua'i specialty that you should not expect to see without considerable time and effort is the very rare and endangered **Puaiohi**. Like all Hawaiian solitaires, the juvenile **Puaiohi** is spotted below. A second solitaire, the larger but similar-looking

Kama'o, survived in very low numbers on Kaua'i until recently, but apparently succumbed to killer Hurricane Iniki in 1992. None has been seen since. It is only the latest in a growing list of species to disappear from Kaua'i's mountain forests, which still harbored all their historically known species as recently as 1970. A particularly tragic loss was the **Kaua'i 'O'o**, a magnificent vocalist and the last member of its family (the honey*eaters*, not to be confused with honey*creepers*) in Hawai'i. The 'o'o survived in the remote Alaka'i Wilderness into the 1970's, when Pratt took the photo shown here. By the early 1980's, it was reduced to a single pair, the female of which disappeared after Hurricane Iwa in 1983. The Kaua'i 'O'o has not been reported since 1987.

Kaua'i 'Elepaio adult   Kaua'i 'Elepaio juvenile

Puaiohi juvenile   Puaiohi

Kaua'i 'O'o • DP

Mamane forest at Puʻu Laʻau • DP

MAUNA KEA'S DRY FOREST

■ Not all of Hawaiʻi's native forests are rain forests. On the Big Island, a distinctive open dry forest high on the leeward slope of Mauna Kea harbors a unique community of native birds. The parklike forest is dominated by the yellow-flowered mamane tree, a member of the pea family. Mamane is the main food source of the endangered **Palila**, a finch-billed honeycreeper that is the crown jewel of the dry montane forest. With its golden-yellow head and breast, the palila blends in beautifully with the mamane blos-soms. It feeds not on nectar, but on seeds. The bird plucks a green seed pod and, holding it against a branch with its feet, rips open a seam to get at the orange-yellow seeds. The mamane forest also supports popu-lations of the "big three," but the **ʻApapane**, and the **ʻIʻiwi**, both of which are stunning among the yel-low flowers, are mostly seasonal vis-itors that follow the blooming cycle. On the other hand, the third mem-ber of the trio, the **Hawaiʻi ʻAmak-ihi**, reaches its greatest population density anywhere in the high

Palila   Palila feeding

Hawai'i 'Amakihi

mamane forest. Probably 90 percent of individual native birds in the forest are Hawai'i 'Amakihi! Sharing the forest with the honeycreepers is a subspecies of **Hawai'i 'Elepaio** that is restricted to this habitat. It is characterized by having much white feathering around the head and in being paler overall than 'elepaios that live in wet forests (see page 52). Often flying high over the entire community is the **Short-eared Owl**. For some reason, the Hawaiian Hawk is only a rare visitor here.

'Apapane

'I'iwi in mamane

Hawai'i 'Elepaio

Short-eared Owl

■ 64

Feral Pig

ALIEN INVADERS STORM THE RAMPARTS

■ Hawai'i's surviving native birds are by no means safe in their mountain retreats. The recent sudden loss of so many birds from the forests of Kaua'ı shows how tenuous a hold the native organisms have on continued existence. Birds that used to ride out the storms-of-the-century such as Hurricane Iniki now cannot do so because valleys that once provided safe refuge are now pestilential death traps. The onslaught of alien organisms, from viruses to mammalian predators, continues to eat away at the islands' biological heritage. Disease-free areas become inexorably smaller and smaller, as mosquitoes adapt to higher and higher elevations. They are aided in their spread by **feral pigs**. The ancient Hawaiian pigs were small, but modern pigs have been "bred up" for improved hunting by release of huge European boars. Pigs plow through the forest undergrowth like animated bulldozers, destroying the native plant cover, opening the ground for invading weeds, and leaving pools ideal for mosquito larvae. The contrast between a pig-damaged forest and a protected one can be striking. On Maui, a native bird called the **Po'o-uli** that was only discovered in 1973 has subsequently been nearly wiped out by pig damage to its understory habitat. (It has never been adequately photographed and is shown in a Pratt painting.) Another insidious threat in the rain forests is the **roof rat**, a far more serious predator than most people realize.

Pig-damaged forest (right)   Roof Rat

House Finch   Po'o-uli • DP

Northwest slope, Haleakala, Maui • DP

DP

DP

DP

It is difficult to realize that the lovely grasslands of today's Hawaiian ranches were created mostly by introduced mammals. When Captain Vancouver presented Kamehameha I with turkeys, he also gave him cattle and goats. Turned loose in the forests, these grazers proved far more effective in converting forest to pasture than outright logging would ever have been. The particularly important mixed forests of koa and ohi'a were especially vulnerable, because saplings of the dominant trees have no defense against grazers. Shown here is a sequence that demonstrates how the prevention of regeneration by grazing destroys a forest without a single tree being logged! As you drive up the slopes of Haleakala on Maui, where groves of exotic eucalyptus dot lush pastures, try to remember that the area was once a koa/ohi'a rain forest alive with native birds. The **House Finches** of today are a poor exchange for parrotbill, 'alauahio, and 'akohekohe.

THE EMBATTLED 'ALALA

■ Historically, Hawai'i was home to only a single member of the widespread crow family, the **Hawaiian Crow** or **'Alala**. Crows worldwide are often thought of as highly adaptable and nearly indestructible birds, but the plight of the Hawaiian species shows that even birds well equipped for survival can stand only so much abuse. Indeed, the 'alala is perhaps the quintessential illustration of what is wrong with Hawaiian ecosystems today. The crow originally had a rather enigmatic distribution, common in the forests of Kona, but absent from seemingly suitable habitats elsewhere on the Big Island. From subfossil remains, we now know that it is the sole survivor of several crow species that once lived throughout the Hawaiian Islands. The others disappeared after the Islands' habitats were altered by the first Polynesian settlers. A small captive flock at the Olinda Endangered Species Facility on Maui was highly inbred and consequently having disappointing breeding success. Now, the McCandless Ranch in South Kona harbors the last three known wild breeding pairs, and heroic efforts are belatedly being made there to save Hawai'i's last crow from extinction.

Hawaiian crows are typical in being large, conspicuous, rambunctious birds that eat a wide variety of foods. They have a huge repertoire of wierd and wonderful vocalizations and, instead of the *caaw* of mainland crows, they utter a loud, high-pitched scream. Up to the 1960's, they remained fairly common around Kona ranches, but they were generally disliked and often shot as a nuisance. Their habit of following pig hunters through the forest and loudly announcing their presence certainly did not endear them to local people, but outright persecution alone cannot explain the bird's sudden decline in recent decades. Studies in the 1970's revealed a severe lack of breeding success. Some eggs and nestlings were taken by rats, and others fledged only to mysteriously disappear. We now know that 'Alala fledglings, before they can fly, spend several days on the ground during which time they are vulnerable to mongooses and feral cats. Also, adult birds are often afflicted with avian malaria and bird pox, although these infections are not always fatal. Add to these threats the ongoing deforestation and other habitat changes, and the outlook for the 'Alala is indeed bleak.

Hawaiian Crow or 'Alala

Following years of bickering among various concerned parties, a new program managed by The Peregrine Fund holds some promise for saving the crow. Biologists remove eggs from wild nests and hatch them in incubators. Some incubator chicks join the captive birds at Olinda, but the rest are released to join the wild flock. Great care is taken to prevent the birds from becoming tame. Hatchlings are fed with crow hand puppets and, when handled,

Olinda Endangered Species Facility Sign • DP

are fitted with falconer's hoods. Once they are old enough, the fledglings are "hacked" into an aviary in the rain forest of McCandless Ranch to acclimate them to the area and allow them to learn to eat natural foods. This period of captivity gets the young birds safely through their vulnerable terrestrial period. Before release, the birds are treated for pox lesions and malaria and fitted with radio transmitters so their movements can be traced. Wild pairs renest after removal of early clutches, but chicks hatched in the wild still have a very low survival rate. By 1994, the second year of the program, the wild population had increased for the first time in years and the captive birds produced the most chicks (at least four) in one season since 1981—results beyond anyone's wildest dreams. Since then, success has been less spectacular, but at least there is now hope that one of Hawai'i's rarest forest birds may live into the next century.

Crow aviary • DP

'Alala with falconer's hood • DP

'Alala foot showing bird pox lesion • DP

'Alala pair feeding in pilo tree

Manana Island, Oahu • DP

HOME PORT FOR OCEAN WANDERERS

◼

*V*isitors are often surprised that Hawai'i has no "seag-ulls." The reason is simple—gulls are scavengers of shallow conti-nental shorelines in mostly temper-ate regions. In fact, the few gulls that do manage to make it to the islands never survive very well. Instead of gulls, Hawai'i is home to members of several families better adapted to feeding in deep, warm waters. Such birds include boobies, terns, tropicbirds, shearwaters, frigatebirds, and albatrosses.

Masked Booby • DP

Outwitting the Predators

■ Seabirds generally require predator-free islands on which to nest. Ground-nesting birds such as the **Masked Booby** breed only on off-shore islands such as Manana off O'ahu, but can be seen flying over the adjacent shoreline. **Sooty Terns** nest in such numbers that from shore they look like a cloud of smoke over an island. At closer range, we can hear their raucous *wide-awake* cries. They sometimes fly inland at night, when their calls may seem a mockery to those trying to sleep. Among the Sooty Terns one can find the **Brown Noddy**, a tern with uncharacteristically dark feathering. Some seabirds avoid predators by nesting off the ground in trees (note that most mongooses are poor climbers, although a few have been observed climbing trees in Kipahulu Valley). The **Red-footed Booby** maintains colonies on both Kaua'i and O'ahu. They feed at sea mostly at night, so can be seen sitting in their colonies all day. The chicks begin life with a fluffy white down that is replaced by a dull gray-brown juvenile plumage by the time the bird fledges. Although the boobies have found ways to thwart ground predators, they still must

Sooty Tern

Brown Noddy

Red-footed Booby

Red-footed Boobies in nest trees • DP

contend with their old nemesis, the **Great Frigatebird**. These graceful scissor-tailed pirates harass incoming boobies to make them disgorge their catch of fish or squid. The frigatebird then catches it before it hits the water. In the breeding season, you might see a male frigatebird with his throat pouch inflated like a red balloon as a display to the female, identified by her white breast.

Red-footed Booby with chick • DP

Red-footed Booby juvenile • DP

Great Frigatebird male • DP

Great Frigatebird female

REFUGE ON THE CLIFFS

■ Other seabirds have solved the predator problem by choosing nest sites on sheer cliffs. The ethereal **White-tailed Tropicbird** is widespread in the islands and even flies over rain forests far inland. It can be seen in such improbable places for a seabird as Kaua'i's Waimea Canyon and the caldera of Kilauea Volcano on the Big Island, where it nests on ledges despite the sulphurous fumes. Local people call them "crater birds." The **Red-tailed Tropicbird** is seen in only a few areas such as Kilauea Point on Kaua'i and Makapu'u on O'ahu, but at both places they put on a spectacular show with their somersaulting flight display involving three birds. Red-tailed tropicbirds nest only on seaward-facing cliffs. Another cliff nester is the **Black Noddy**. Look for it along Kaua'i's Na Pali Coast or the sea cliffs of Hawaii Volcanoes National Park. It is similar to the brown noddy but is smaller, darker, and has a contrasting gray tail as an adult.

White-tailed Tropicbird • DP

Red-tailed Tropicbird • DP

Black Noddy • DP

UNDERGROUND SEABIRDS

■ It is a surprise to many that some seabirds, such as shearwaters and petrels that spend most of their lives in exuberant flight over open seas, begin life in holes in the ground. That is indeed the case for one of Hawai'i's commonest seabirds, the **Wedge-tailed Shearwater**. If you go fishing offshore, you are sure to see these mouse-gray birds coursing low over the waves on stiffly held wings. They do indeed seem to shear the water with their wingtips. For nesting, wedge-tails choose offshore islets or the tips of promontories on the main islands that provide a degree of protection from predators. A typical site that is also a good place to observe their habits is **Kilauea Point National Wildlife Refuge** on Kaua'i. Although the parent birds come and go mostly at dawn and dusk, a few can be seen on the ground during midday. The fluffy gray chicks hunkered down in their cozy burrows are a delight. At night, the birds fill the air with eerie braying cries that might seem ghostly to the uninformed. **Newell's Shearwater** also nests in burrows, but these are in scattered localities high in the mountains, with most of the population on Kaua'i. When their chicks fledge in the fall, they leave their burrows at night and follow an innate drive to fly toward the brightest part of the sky (which used to be the distant horizon or the moon—in either case toward the sea, away from the island). Nowadays, however, the bright lights of towns and resorts confuse many birds, especially on cloudy nights, and the birds rain down on lawns and parking lots. Many are killed each year by cars, cats, and dogs. Shearwater feet are placed for swimming, and the birds cannot walk on, or take off from, level ground. They are not injured, but need a helping hand. If you find a grounded shearwater, take it to the nearest fire station, where it will be kept for safe release.

Wedge-tailed Shearwater • DP

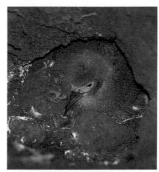

Wedge-tailed Shearwater chick • DP

Kilauea Point National Wildlife Refuge • DP

Wedge-tailed Shearwater adult

Newell's Shearwater • DP

Return of the Albatross

Laysan Albatross

Laysan Albatrosses displaying

■ The largest and in many ways most impressive of seabirds are the albatrosses. Until the past two decades, albatrosses have been long gone from the main Hawaiian Islands, although they continued to nest in large numbers on the uninhabited islands that stretch west to Kure Atoll. Then, a few pairs of **Laysan Albatross** began attempting to nest on Kaua'i and O'ahu, initially with little success because dogs always got their chicks. With help from man, however, a thriving colony has become established at Kilauea Point, where they put on one of the best wildlife shows in the islands. Courtship begins in December when pairs engage in their bowing and strutting display, accompanied by weird braying and whistling. Later, the dumpy gray-brown chicks provide a striking contrast to their sleek parents. Even the adults are not very graceful on the ground and often end their magnificent fixed-wing flights with a crash-landing. Such comical behavior earned them the nickname "gooney bird."

Laysan Albatross parent with chick

AN AVIAN MISCELLANY

●

*Y*ou have met most of Hawai'i's conspicuous and common birds, plus many of the Islands' rare native species, in previous sections. Some have been overlooked, however, so here we present a selection of these species, plus a few others that need further comment. We have made no effort to be complete. For complete lists of the birds of Hawai'i, consult the references on p. 108.

Pied-billed Grebe. Hawai'i's single small colony of this ducklike waterbird inhabits 'Aimakapa Pond near Kailua-Kona on the Big Island. The grebes first appeared there in the early 1980s and, if they survive long-term, will represent the only successful natural colonization of Hawai'i in historic times.

DP

DP

Black-footed Albatross. Although abundant in nesting colonies on the uninhabited Northwestern Hawaiian Islands, this albatross is only occasionally seen among the main islands. They can sometimes be seen from shore, but a better bet is to take a fishing boat out to sea.

Christmas Shearwater. This all-dark shearwater was discovered by Captain Cook on Christmas Day, hence the unusual name. The species is rare in Hawai'i, but nests on a few islets off O'ahu including Moku Manu, the small rocky island off the tip of Mokapu Peninsula in Kane'ohe. A careful observer with a telescope can pick out a few Christmas Shearwaters among the thousands of Wedge-tails as they return to nesting sites at dusk.

DP

Masked Booby. The largest and rarest of Hawai'i's three boobies, the Masked is regularly seen only on O'ahu. It nests in low numbers on Moku Manu, off the tip of Mokapu Peninsula. They are more common on the uninhabited Northwestern Hawaiian Islands. Photo on p. 72.

Brown Booby. *Sula leucogaster.* The handsome Brown Booby is a common sight flying offshore and perching on buoys. Good places to look for them include Waikiki, Honolulu Harbor, and the North Shore beaches on O'ahu, and Kilauea Point on Kaua'i. They nest on offshore islets and are present all year in Hawai'i.

DP

Migratory Ducks used to be abundant in the Hawaiian Islands, but overhunting in the 1800s and conversion of natural wetlands to other purposes has reduced their numbers drastically. The Northern Pintail and Northern Shoveler (p. 41) are still fairly common, but the other regular visitors are never numerous. Hawai'i receives an interesting mix of Eurasian and American waterfowl. "Dabbling" ducks are represented by both American and Eurasian Wigeons and both races of **Green-winged Teal**, the Garganey, and the American **Blue-winged Teal**. Among the "diving" ducks, the most common is the **Lesser Scaup**, but each winter sees them joined by a few Tufted Ducks, a common Old World species, as well as **Ring-necked Ducks** from North America.

Green-winged Teal • DP

Blue-winged Teal • DP

Lesser Scaup • DP

Ring-necked Duck • DP

Osprey. If you are anywhere other than the Big Island and see a soaring raptor, you are probably seeing an Osprey. This cosmopolitan fish-eating bird winters in low numbers every year in the Hawaiian Islands. Ospreys are much larger than Hawaiian Hawks, and are almost always seen near water. If you are lucky, you may see one plunge feet-first into the water to catch a fish, then emerge and take off with its prey dangling in its talons.

DP

Wild Turkey. Hawai'i's Wild Turkeys (p. 29) have the distinction of being the first bird introduced to the Islands by non-Polynesians. The initial introduction has been augmented many times, so that today the population is a genetic amalgam of several subspecies. Some birds show the chestnut tail feather tips characteristic of birds from eastern North America, others have white tips like those of Mexican birds that were the ancestors of domestic turkeys, and many are intermediate.

Common Pheasant. Pheasants were introduced to Hawai'i in the 19th century for ornament and sport. The familiar ring-necked form is a common sight in ranch lands and open fields on all islands. In wetter habitats on the Big Island, the Japanese subspecies shown here, often called the "Green Pheasant," replaces the more familiar ring-neck. The two interbreed freely where they come into contact, and many intermediates are present on the island.

DP

DP

California Quail. These small game birds with their unusual topknots were introduced to Hawai'i first in the 1850s. Today, they are most often seen in rocky or grassy places on ranch lands of the Big Island. Their *chi-ca-go* calls, often heard in the background of Hollywood movies, are now part of the sounds of the tropical Pacific. The closely related Gambel's Quail has also been introduced, but is much rarer.

DP

Semipalmated Plover. Although rare compared to the ubiquitous Pacific Golden-Plover (p. 18), the smaller Semipalmated is the second most common plover to visit Hawai'i. It keeps to mudflats and wetlands where it associates with other shorebirds. It is characterized by its plain upperparts and single breast band.

Lesser Yellowlegs. One of the larger shorebirds in Hawai'i, the appropriately named Lesser Yellowlegs is an annual winter visitor in low numbers. Look for it in grassy areas near wetlands. Note that the yellowlegs is much taller than the more common Wandering Tattler (p. 37), which also has yellow legs.

DP

DP

Least Sandpiper. This is the most common of the small sandpipers called "peeps" that winter in Hawai'i. It is brown in all plumages and has yellow legs, but is much smaller than the Lesser Yellowlegs (see above). Like many other sandpipers and plovers, this species nests in the arctic and "vacations" during the winter in warmer climes. In Hawai'i, it inhabits mudflats in places such as canefield settling basins and aquaculture ponds.

Long-billed Dowitcher. Dowitchers are squat, long-billed sandpipers that feed by an up-and-down sewing-machine motion. Two species visit Hawai'i, but the Short-billed Dowitcher is very rare. In Hawai'i, dowitchers are usually found in small flocks, easily identified by a longitudinal slash of white down the back, visible in flight. Look for them in any good shorebird habitat.

Common Snipe. Victims of the old "snipe hunt" trick may think there is no such bird, but snipes are very real and are rare winter visitors to Hawai'i. They live in grassy wetlands such as those of the James Campbell National Wildlife Refuge and are less likely to be seen in the open than other shorebirds. They are hard to spot on the ground, and are usually discovered as they flush from cover with a loud call that sounds rather like tearing cloth.

DP

Pomarine Jaeger. Jaegers are large, dark, gull-like seabirds that breed in the high arctic, where they are important predators on young birds. In their winter quarters, which for this species includes waters around the Hawaiian Islands, they tend to be scavengers. Local fishermen, who often see these birds just outside Honolulu Harbor, call them "garbage birds."

DP

Why No "Seagulls?" The answer to one of the most frequently asked questions about birds in Hawai'i is a bit complex. And while Hawai'i's harbors, unlike those on the mainland, do not ring with the cries of gulls, it is not entirely true that Hawai'i has no gulls. Note that there is no species called "Sea Gull." This is a colloquial term that applies to dozens of gull species, many of which visit the Islands on rare occasions. Frequently such visitors are stranded waifs that eventually starve to death in the poor habitat. Gulls are mostly scavengers of shallow, temperate coastal waters. The Hawaiian Islands rise abruptly from the depths of the sea, and lack anything comparable to a continental shelf. Around the world, few gulls live in tropical seas. One that does, the **Laughing Gull** shown here (above), is also one of the most frequent visitors to Hawai'i. Laughing Gulls breed on both coasts of Middle America. They have an all-black head during the nesting season, but most birds in Hawai'i are pale-headed. Of the gulls that reach Hawai'i from temperate areas, the most often seen is the **Ring-billed Gull** (right), but Bonaparte's, Herring, California, Western, and Glaucous-winged gulls show up occasionally.

DP

DP

Gray-backed Tern. Although it is common in the Northwestern Hawaiian Islands and elsewhere in the tropical Pacific, this tern is neither common nor widespread in the main islands. A single breeding colony exists on Moku Mahu off Kane'ohe, O'ahu. Birds from that colony disperse widely around the island and can be seen from boats offshore. They sometimes fly close enough to be observed from land, when their paler upper parts separate them from the more common Sooty Terns (p. 74).

Chestnut-bellied Sandgrouse. Sandgrouse are flocking birds of the deserts of Africa and Asia, and are more closely related to pigeons and doves than to true grouse. This species was introduced to the Big Island earlier this century as a potential game bird. Hawai'i seems a strange place for sandgrouse, but they seem to have found the dry grasslands of South

DP

Kohala to be similar enough to their African homelands. Although well established in that small area, sandgrouse have never become a major game bird for Hawaiian hunters.

Barn Owl. Hawai'i's "other" owl was introduced from mainland North America in the 1950s. It is now found on all the main islands where it feeds primarily on introduced rodents. There is some evidence that they also take young birds, such as Laysan Albatross chicks at Kilauea Point (p. 80). Barn Owls often roost in abandoned buildings during the day, and are much more nocturnal than the native Short-eared Owl.

'Elepaio. Hawai'i's native flycatchers belong to a family known as monarchs that mostly inhabit the Australian region. Until recently, they were regarded as the one native forest bird that seemed not to have suffered at the hand of man. But things have changed and, while 'Elepaio can still be seen in the forests of Kaua'i and the Big Island, the O'ahu form, shown here, has declined drastically since the 1970s and is now a candidate for listing as an Endangered Species. Some recent authors have suggested that the Kaua'i, O'ahu, and Hawai'i 'Elepaios be considered separate species.

DP

Northern Mockingbird. Visitors from the mainland U. S. may be surprised to see

DP

or hear this old friend from back home. Mockingbirds in Hawai'i are never particularly common, but can be found on all islands in drier habitats. Their repertoire in the islands is limited, possibly because they have fewer species to mimic.

Western Meadowlark. One of the more unexpected introductions to Hawai'i is this common bird of the grasslands of western North America. It is found only on Kaua'i, where it can be seen in fields that resemble its preferred habitat in its natural range. Coincidentally and ironically, the Western Meadowlark's song somewhat resembles that of the recently extinct Kaua'i 'O'o. Most would consider it a poor exchange.

DP

Kaua'i 'Amakihi. Until recently, all 'amakihis were considered to belong to a single species. Recently, however, this and the following species have been shown to be different from the Hawai'i 'Amakihi found from Moloka'i to the Big Island. The Kaua'i 'Amakihi has a much larger bill than the others, as well as different feeding behavior and distinctive vocalizations.

O'ahu 'Amakihi. See above species. This O'ahu specialty is actually still easy to see in the forests behind the city of Honolulu. Good places to look include the Tantalus/Roundtop loop and Lyon Arboretum. This species differs from other 'amakihis in that males are much yellower below, and females are drab with prominent pale wing bars.

DP

House Sparrow. Because of its close association with human activities, this European sparrow has been called the "feathered mouse." It is now widespread in cities worldwide. In Hawai'i, it has been nicknamed "hamburger sparrow" because it is so often seen around fast-food restaurants. It is a truly urban bird that is only rarely seen in forests, but it also can be abundant around domestic animals on ranches.

Black-rumped Waxbill. If you see what looks like a Common Waxbill (p. 33) on the Big Island, you are probably seeing this species instead. Although not certainly established until recently, it has become fairly abundant and easy to find in the Pu'u Anahulu area of South Kohala. Like its cousin on O'ahu, it feeds in roadside grasses when the seeds are still green.

DP

Red Avadavat or Strawberry Waxbill. These charming little finches are now abundant in grassy open habitats on both O'ahu and the Big Island. The name is a corruption of Ahmadabad, a city in India whence the birds were first exported, so the pronunciation is *AH-vah-dah-VAHT*. The alternative name certainly seems more appropriate and is certainly easier to pronounce. Adult males, with their all-red body feathers speckled with white, do indeed look like animated strawberries.

Chestnut Mannikin. These tiny birds are common in grassy places and along roadsides on O'ahu and Kaua'i. They often flock with other waxbills and small finches but are darker than most with distinctive rich chestnut body plumage. Their disproportionally large blue bills are another noticeable feature. On Kaua'i, they may form huge swarms of hundreds of birds in the edges of sugar cane fields, but can also be seen on the lawns of resorts and even at the Lihu'e airport.

HAWAI‘I'S ENDANGERED AND THREATENED BIRDS

━

*W*ell over half of the birds on the Federal list of Endangered and Threatened Species are Hawaiian! Some birds still so listed are now almost certainly extinct, and others, once common, are being studied as possible additions to the list. Programs of habitat preservation and captive breeding are being carried out by the federal and state governments and private organizations such as The Nature Conservancy of Hawai‘i and The Peregrine Fund in an effort to save these species, but the trend is not in the birds' favor. In this section we review these hapless birds and some of the reasons for their present sad condition.

Hawaiian Petrel. Endangered. This handsome black-and-white seabird nests only in rocky burrows, such as the one shown here, high in the mountains of the Hawaiian Islands where they are under constant threat from ground predators such as feral cats and mongooses. A closely related species lives in the Galapagos Islands. The Hawaiian name *'ua'u* imitates the calls the birds make as they fly above their colony sites at night.

DP

Newell's Shearwater. Threatened. Like the Hawaiian Petrel, Newell's Shearwater nests only in the mountains of the Hawaiian Islands. The shearwater, however, prefers heavily vegetated rather than rocky sites. The largest colonies are on Kaua‘i, where some are protected in preserves of The Nature Conservancy. Photo on p. 79.

DP

Nene or Hawaiian Goose. Endangered. The State Bird is actually the lone survivor of a community of grazing waterfowl that inhabited the Islands before the coming of the Polynesians. We know the other species from their bones that have recently been found in caves, lava tubes, and other such places. The Nene survived probably because it was the only species that had not lost the power of flight.

Hawaiian Duck or Koloa. Endangered. The relationship of the native duck to the familiar Mallard is obvious, but the Hawaiian birds are noticeably smaller and have no bright male plumage. Mallards are found all over Hawai'i, mostly as birds kept for ornament. Given the choice, the native ducks tend not to associate with Mallards, but when their numbers are

DP

low and mates are scarce, hybridization is inevitable. Nearly all supposed Hawaiian Ducks on O'ahu have some Mallard ancestry, but genetically pure birds are still found on Kaua'i.

DP

Laysan Duck. Endangered. This unusual duck lives only on the tiny remote island of Laysan in the Northwestern Hawaiian Islands. The small population centers around the saline lake in the middle of the island and feeds on, among other things, brine flies. The ducks' continued existence depends on preservation of the habitat and preventing the spread of ground predators to the island.

Hawaiian Hawk. Threatened. Shown on pp. 31 and 53, the resident native hawk is a small raptor that feeds mostly on large insects and rodents. Before humans brought mice and rats to Hawai'i, the hawks probably took more birds. Once considered Endangered, the hawk's status has been changed because it appears to be maintaining a stable population.

Hawaiian Common Moorhen. Endangered. Although this species is found nearly world wide and is often common, the distinctive Hawaiian subspecies has suffered the same fate as other Hawaiian wetland birds because of habitat loss. Today, it is found mostly on Kaua'i and O'ahu. The moorhen is shier and more likely to hide in vegetation than the Hawaiian Coot.

DP

Hawaiian Coot. Endangered. Closely related to the familiar American Coot, the Hawaiian species differs in the size and shape of the knob on the front of its head. Hawaiian Coots are more numerous than other native water-birds, partly because they have a broader range of habitats that includes estuaries and ocean bays. They can be seen throughout the islands in suitable places.

Hawaiian Black-necked Stilt. Endangered. Some authorities consider the Hawaiian Stilt a subspecies of the mainland Black-necked, and some classify it a separate species. Either way, it has suffered the same fate as Hawai'i's other native freshwater birds because of habitat loss. Stilts were probably one of the few species to benefit by the arrival of the first Hawaiians. Ancient taro fields provided ample habitat, but today such wetlands are few and far between. Interestingly, the stilt is the only "shorebird" to breed in the Hawaiian Islands; all others are non-breeding visitors.

DP

Bristle-thighed Curlew. Endangered. Only recently added to the list of Endangered Species, this curlew is primarily a spring and fall passage migrant in the main Hawaiian Islands, but many winter in the Northwestern Hawaiian Islands that make up the Hawaiian Islands National Wildlife Refuge. Bristle-thighed Curlews undergo a moult on their wintering grounds that renders them flightless for several days, when they are highly vulnerable to ground predators. Consequently, they can winter safely only on remote uninhabited islands. Photo on p. 37.

Hawaiian Crow or 'Alala. Endangered. The Hawaiian Crow (pp. 68-71) clearly qualifies as one of the world's rarest birds. For many years, birders had no chance of seeing this bird in the wild, but now not only are the heroic conservation efforts on the crow's behalf paying off, but the McCandless Ranch has instigated an ecotour program (see Birding Hotspots, p. 103) that provides an opportunity to see these spectacular birds in beautiful native rain forests.

Kama'o. Endangered, possibly extinct. Hawaiian thrushes are related to the solitaires of North and South America. The Kama'o, the larger of Kaua'i's two species, was the most similar of all to mainland solitaires. It was at one time the island's most abundant native bird. Now it is apparently gone (p. 60 and below). The Kama'o had a spectacular song comprising flute-like cascades of notes, buzzy sounds, and trills. It can be heard on *Voices of Hawaii's Birds* (see p. 108).

DP

Puaiohi. Endangered. The smaller of Kaua'i's solitaires was always considered rare, but today survives while its larger and more historically common relative may not. The reason has to do with the way the two coexisted. The Puaiohi seems to be a bird of deep ravines, whereas the Kama'o inhabited the higher plateaus and ridge tops. During the recent hurricanes, the Puaiohi could ride out the storm "at home," but the Kama'o followed their traditional instincts and evacuated to lowland valleys, now infested with disease-carrying mosquitoes. Because of man's alteration of the environment, what used to be a successful survival strategy became a liability. More photos on p. 61.

Oloma'o. Endangered, possibly extinct. This native solitaire, which looks much like the 'Oma'o (p.52), once inhabited both Lana'i and Moloka'i but now survives, if at all, only on the latter. The last confirmed sighting was in 1988 in The Nature Conservancy's Kamakou Preserve. The reasons for its decline are not specifically known, but are probably the same as those for other native forest birds.

Kaua'i 'O'o. Extinct. Although it has not yet been removed from the list of Endangered Species, this beautiful singer no longer initiates the dawn chorus on Kaua'i. The last known individual disappeared sometime after 1987, and diligent searches have failed to find any more. You can hear the haunting song of the Kaua'i 'O'o on *Voices of Hawaii's Birds* (see p. 108). Photo on p. 61.

Laysan Finch and **Nihoa Finch.** Endangered. These two finchlike Hawaiian honeycreepers are confined to their namesake islands in the remote Northwestern Hawaiian Islands chain. They are under no imminent threat, but any species confined to a tiny island is inherently vulnerable to changes in its environment. The Laysan Finch demonstrated remarkable resilience by living on seabird eggs to survive the destruction of Laysan's vegetation by introduced rabbits earlier this century. An introduced population at Midway Atoll, however, succumbed quickly when rats got ashore there during World War II.

'O'u. Endangered. At one time, this was one of the most common Hawaiian honeycreepers throughout the islands (p. 51). It survived into the 1980s on the Big Island and Kaua'i, but it has not been reliably reported since then on Hawai'i and may not have survived

Hurricane Iniki on Kaua'i, although one possible sighting has been made since then. The 'O'u had a loud musical song and humanlike upslurred whistle calls. It was not primarily a bird of high elevations, and most of its preferred habitat now lies within the mosquito zone.

Palila. Endangered. This is the only finchlike Hawaiian honeycreeper that birders in the main Hawaiian Islands have any chance to see. The population of a few thousand birds lives only in the mamane forest on the upper slopes of Mauna Kea (p. 62). After two centuries of habitat degradation by feral sheep, goats, and cattle, the mamane forest is now being protected for this very interesting native bird.

Maui Parrotbill. Endangered. This unique Hawaiian honeycreeper is a Maui endemic (p. 56). It is one of the few rare Hawaiian birds to have been observed more often in recent years than formerly. It was not reported in the 20th century before 1950, but now is seen regularly in the Waikamoi Preserve (p. 101) and other wilderness areas of East Maui. This may reflect an increase in observers rather than an increase in parrotbills. More photos on p. 57.

Nukupu'u. Endangered. This bird is an ornithological enigma. It seems to be able to hang on for many years at very low numbers, and competent observers (including the author!) have never seen one. It has been rare since the last century and is extinct on O'ahu, but has been seen recently on both Kaua'i and Maui (by Jack Jeffrey, among others). Sightings tend to be widely spaced in time and unrepeatable. No one has ever been able to "stake out" a Nukupu'u, and its breeding habits and voice are essentially unknown. The bird is closely related to the Big Island 'Akiapola'au, but differs in having a weaker curved lower bill.

'Akiapola'au. Endangered. This unique bird is discussed in detail on pp. 10-11. It can still be observed in remote forests on the Big Island, such as those preserved in Hakalau Forest National Wildlife Refuge (p. 105). Why this species has done better than the closely related Nukupu'u is a matter of speculation.

O'ahu 'Alauahio. Endangered, probably extinct. This O'ahu endemic, which resembles the Maui 'Alauahio (pp. 6, 57), has not been reliably reported for over a decade. It survived in low numbers into the mid-20th century, but sightings gradually ceased. Hope remains that a few may survive in some seldom-visited valley. It is not a conspicuous bird and looks enough like an O'ahu 'Amakihi that one would have to be looking for it specifically to find it.

Hawai'i Creeper. Endangered. Although it is nowhere common, the creeper still is widely distributed on Hawai'i. Its continued survival depends on preservation of montane forests such as those of Hakalau Forest National Wildlife Refuge (p. 105). Hawai'i Creepers are often mistaken for 'Amakihi by beginners, but their pale, nearly straight bills and nuthatch-like habits identify them.

'Akepa. Endangered. This brilliant orange honeycreeper was once found on O'ahu, Maui, and Hawai'i. It is certainly extinct on O'ahu, and critically endangered on Maui. On the Big Island, it is doing somewhat better and is actually common in remote forests such as Hakalau Forest National Wildlife Refuge (p. 105). Lucky observers may also see it in *kipukas* along the Saddle Road.

'Akohekohe or Crested Honeycreeper.
Endangered. A large and spectacular
Hawaiian honeycreeper, this species is still
locally common in the remote wilderness
of East Maui. It formerly lived on Moloka'i
as well. It is a nectar-feeder dependent on
'ohi'a-lehua flowers. Its weird, low-pitched
vocalizations sound rather like recordings
played back too slowly. Lucky observers
may see this species in The Nature
Conservancy's Waikamoi Preserve (p. 101).

Po'o-uli. Endangered. Amazingly, this dull brown black-faced bird escaped
detection by early ornithologists in Hawai'i. It was first described in 1974 by
students from the University of Hawai'i who had discovered it the previous
year in the remote wilderness of East Maui. Since then, the discovery site has
been trashed by feral pigs, and the birds can no longer be found there. A few
survive in other places, but pigs are moving into those areas as well.
Obviously, the survival of this extremely interesting bird depends on control
of these alien mammals. Photo on p. 66.

Po'o-uli habitat, East Maui •DP

A DOZEN BIRDING HOTSPOTS

■

$\mathcal{T}$he following birding sites were selected from many potential ones because they are places the visitor is likely go, are easily accessible, are especially rich in species, have special birds than can be seen nowhere else, or a combination of these factors. The descriptions here are necessarily brief. The serious birder will want to consult *Enjoying Birds in Hawai'i* (see p. 108), a detailed bird-finding guide to these and many other sites.

1. Kilauea Point and Hanalei National Wildlife Refuges, Kaua'i. These two refuges on Kaua'i's North Shore are administered jointly. Kilauea Point has become one of the island's most popular tourist attractions. It is ideal for viewing and photographing seabirds at close range. Birds that breed at the point include Red-footed Booby, Wedge-tailed Shearwater, Laysan Albatross, and Red-tailed Tropicbird. This may be the best and most accessible place in the world for the latter species. White-tailed Tropicbirds and Great Frigatebirds are also commonly seen at Kilauea, as are recently reintroduced

Nene. The refuge is open during specified hours (inquire before you visit) and a nominal admission is charged. Hanalei Refuge preserves an active taro farm as well as other ponds that provide habitat for all of Hawai'i's native freshwater birds. An overlook along the highway affords a breathtaking panoramic view of the refuge and the Hanalei River, and a narrow public road passes closer to the ponds. For further information, contact the Refuge Manager (P. O. Box 87, Kilauea HI 96754).

2. Koke'e Area, Kaua'i. This area, located at the northwestern end of Hwy. 550 on Kaua'i, encompasses three state parks (Waimea Canyon, Na Pali Coast, and Koke'e), two natural area reserves, and the Alaka'i Wilderness Preserve, all administered by the State of Hawai'i. All places are open to the public, but overnight stays are not permitted in wilderness areas. Amidst some of Hawai'i's most spectacular scenery, birders can view a host of native species, including White-tailed Tropicbird, Pacific Golden-Plover, Short-eared Owl, Kaua'i 'Elepaio, 'Apapane, 'I'iwi, Kaua'i 'Amakihi, 'Anianiau, 'Akeke'e, and for the lucky, 'Akikiki. All except the last-men-

tioned can be seen right along the public highway or around overlooks, where they are joined by such introduced species as Erckel's Francolin, Red Junglefowl, White-rumped Shama, Melodious Laughing-thrush, and Northern Cardinal. For a better chance at 'Akikiki and such rarities as Puaiohi, one must do some hiking off Mohihi Road (four-wheel-drive only) which begins in Koke'e State Park. David Kuhn of Terran Tours (Box 1018, Waimea HI 96796; 808/335-3313) can outfit your wilderness expedition. A small museum at Koke'e State Park offers books on natural

DP

history and maps of the area, the latter essential for hikers. Koke'e Lodge (P. O. Box 819, Waimea HI 96796) offers rustic housekeeping cabins at modest rates.

3. Kapi'olani Park, O'ahu. At the foot of Diamond Head at the east end of Waikiki, this urban park is an excellent place for a visitor to become acquainted with the commoner birds of Hawai'i. Although most of the species here are introduced, they are joined by native Pacific

Golden-Plovers, Common Fairy-Terns, Great Frigatebirds (overhead), and Brown Boobies (offshore). In the ironwood trees near the fountain at the east end, live Yellow-fronted Canary, House Finch, Java Sparrow, Red-crested and Northern Cardinal, and both bulbuls. White-rumped Shamas can be found in trees on the mauka side, and unmowed grassy places may have Nutmeg Mannikins and Common Waxbills.

4. Kahuku Area, O'ahu. This area lies at the northernmost tip of O'ahu, a strategic landfall for migratory shorebirds, ducks, gulls, and others. The area's ponds serve as "migrant traps" that are among the most exciting places to look for rarities in the Hawaiian Islands. The ponds also serve as breeding grounds for native moorhens, coots, stilts, and ducks. Bristle-thighed Curlews are regular here August-October, and this is perhaps the best place on O'ahu to find Short-eared Owls. Regular shorebird visitors, especially in the fall, include Sharp-tailed and Pectoral Sandpipers, Long-billed Dowitchers, Lesser Yellowlegs, and even Common Snipe. Hawai'i's common winter ducks (p. 41) are often joined here by both Eurasian and American Wigeon, Green-winged and Blue-winged Teal, Garganey, and Tufted Duck. Although not primarily a place for land birds, the area features large flocks of Red Avadavats, Chestnut Mannikins, and Common Waxbills and Japanese Bush-warblers are abundant

DP

in thickets. The heart of the area is the James Campbell National Wildlife Refuge at the northern edge of the village of Kahuku with a detached section around Punamano Pond a few miles north. Adjacent to the refuge along the main highway is a now-defunct aquafarm whose drained ponds provide additional shorebird habitat. Many of the refuge's breeding birds can be seen in these ponds from the highway. The main part of the refuge is closed during the nesting season (February-August), and gates are usually locked, but plans are being made to increase public access. A few persons have permits to take visitors onto the refuge. For the latest information, contact the Refuge Manager at P. O. Box 340, Hale'iwa HI 96712 or (808) 637-6330. A few miles south in the town of La'ie is La'ie Point, a good spot from which to scope for seabirds during spring and summer.

5. Kanaha and Kealia Ponds, Maui. Located in the narrow isthmus that separates East and West Maui are two ponds that provide important habitat for native freshwater birds as well as wintering waterfowl and migratory shorebirds. Both are readily accessible from major highways. The ponds are only a few miles apart "as the crow flies," so considerable interchange occurs. Nearly every winter, one or two Ospreys work these ponds, and they are the best places on Maui to look for rarities. Kanaha Pond, located between the airport and Kahului, is a state sanctuary with a parking lot and observation shelter. Hawaiian Stilts, Hawaiian Coots, and Black-crowned Night-Herons are used to visitors here and allow close approach for photography. Recently established Kealia

DP

Pond National Wildlife Refuge lies along Highway 31, between Kihei and Highway 30. At several points one can easily walk to the edge of the pond from the highway. Because Kealia is a large pond, a spotting scope is useful. Visitor activities and facilities are still under development. The pond has both deep water favored by diving ducks and mudflats important for shorebirds. Cattle Egrets have a large roost in the trees on the far side. Kealia is one of the most reliable places for Black-bellied Plovers and Sharp-tailed Sandpipers in the fall, and also attracts smaller sandpipers such as Least and Western. For the latest information on the new refuge, write to the Refuge Manager, Kealia Pond National Wildlife Refuge, Box 1042, Kihei HI 96753.

6. Haleakala National Park and Waikamoi Preserve, Maui. No visitor to Maui should miss the drive to Haleakala (*HA-lay-ah-kah-LAH*, not *Holly-ockle-a*) Crater. The trip offers not only spectacular scenery, but also some excellent birding. On the way up, Short-eared Owls, Common Pheasants, and Eurasian Skylarks are conspicuous. The road between park headquarters and the summit area is good for Nene and Chukar, and the main Hawaiian Petrel nesting colony lies just below the upper visitor center. The only accessible area in the park for forest birds is Hosmer Grove, to the left just past the entrance kiosk. A short trail here should produce 'Apapane, 'I'iwi, Hawai'i 'Amakihi, Maui 'Alauahio, Red-billed Leiothrix, House Finch, Northern Cardinal, and Melodious Laughing-thrush. Hosmer Grove is the starting point for hikes into The Nature

Conservancy's Waikamoi Preserve, adjacent to the park. Waikamoi has all the same species plus such rarities as 'Akohekohe and Maui Parrotbill. Hikes into Waikamoi are conducted by both the Conservancy and the National Park Service. The park charges an entrance fee. For the latest schedules and other information contact The Superintendent, Haleakala National Park, Box 369, Makawao HI 96768; or Preserve Manager, Waikamoi Preserve, Box 1716, Makawao HI 96768-1716.

7. 'Aimakapa Pond, Hawai'i. This ancient fishpond, pronounced *EYE-mah-kah-PAH*, lies within Kaloko-Honokohau National Historical Park just north of Honokohau Boat Harbor between Kailua-Kona and Keahole Airport. It is the only place in the Hawaiian Islands where Pied-billed Grebes nest. Along with the grebes are Hawaiian Stilts, Hawaiian Coots, and Black-crowned Night-Herons. In the woods and lava flows nearby, Red-crested Cardinal, Saffron Finch, Warbling Silverbill, and Lavender Waxbill can be found. From September through April, 'Aimakapa is a wonderful "migrant trap" that has produced numerous rarities over the years. The pond usually has a good winter population of shovelers and pintails, along with both wigeons, Ring-necked Duck, Blue-winged and Green-winged Teal, and Lesser Scaup. The lava flows and beaches on the ocean side of the pond are good places for tattlers, turnstones, Sanderlings, and plovers. Almost anything could turn up here. For the latest information and directions, write to The Superintendent, Kaloko-

DP

Honokohau National Historical Park, 73-4786 Kanalani St., #14, Kailua-Kona HI 96740 or call (808) 329-6881.

8. McCandless Ranch, Hawai'i. This privately owned area has only recently become accessible to birders, and so it is not included in *Enjoying Birds in Hawai'i.* A 45-minute drive south of Kailua-Kona, the ranch offers an ecotour as well as a lovely bed-and-breakfast facility on one of Hawai'i's historic ranches. The main

DP

attraction, of course, is the last wild flock of Hawaiian Crows. No guarantees of success are made, but the ranch guides are very good at finding the birds without disturbing them. The tour also includes some beautiful native rain forests where one can expect to see 'Apapane, 'I'iwi, Hawai'i 'Amakihi, Hawai'i 'Elepaio, Hawaiian Hawk, and Kalij Pheasant. The tours are not cheap, but considering that this is the only chance one has to see one of the world's rarest birds, they are reasonable. For up-to-date information and prices, write to McCandless Ranch Ecotour, Box 500, Honaunau HI 96726, or call (808) 328-8246.

9. Pu'u Wa'a Wa'a Area, Hawai'i. One of Hawai'i's most productive birding areas, in terms of number of species, lies along Mamalahoa Highway (180) between Kailua-Kona and Waimea at the base of the prominent cinder cone called Pu'u Wa'a Wa'a. Most of the land is private, but public roads provide sufficient access. The area includes a remnant of native lowland dry forest. Close to the entrance to Pu'u Wa'a Wa'a Ranch, the road makes a sharp turn and climbs the side of a ridge called Pu'u Anahulu. A pull-out near the top of the hill provides a good place to park and bird the roadside. Closer to Waimea, a new subdivision called Pu'u Lani Ranch affords excellent roadside birding without heavy traffic. The area features four native birds (Nene, Hawaiian Hawk, Short-eared Owl, and Hawai'i 'Amakihi) as well as a host of

introduced game birds and finches. The Nene often hang around the stables at Pu'u Lani, and are quite tame. Other large ground-dwelling birds include Wild Turkey, Common Peafowl, Kalij Pheasant, and both Erckel's and Black Francolins. In open woods with tall grasses, look for Saffron Finch, Yellow-fronted Canary, Red-cheeked Cordonbleu, Warbling Silverbill, and Lavender Waxbill. In more open areas and along roadsides, Black-rumped Waxbills, Nutmeg Mannikins, and Red Avadavats often form large flocks. Water sources such as lawn sprinklers attract many birds in this usually dry region.

10. Pu'u La'au, Hawai'i. This site, administered by the State of Hawai'i, includes portions of both Ka'ohe Game Management Area and Mauna Kea Forest Reserve. It is the only place where one can see the endangered Palila, but it features many other interesting species as well. It is reached via an all-weather gravel road off the Saddle Road between Waiki'i and Pohakuloa. The road is unmarked, but can be recognized by the hunter registration kiosk at the entrance and a large cinder cone (Ahumoa) visible upslope. The public road leads to the Pu'u La'au cabin about six miles up. The road goes further, but requires four-wheel-drive beyond the cabin. During the spring months, Palila can be found anywhere above Ahumoa, with the area around the cabin being especially productive. Later in the year the birds become quiet and tend to move to higher elevations, so they can be difficult to find. Also in the area

is a distinctive pale subspecies of Hawai'i 'Elepaio and an incredibly high population of Hawai'i 'Amakihi. Short-eared Owls are often seen, and when the mamane trees are in bloom, 'I'iwi and 'Apapane visit the area. For the very lucky, the 'Akiapola'au is a rare resident. Introduced small birds include Skylark, Yellow-fronted Canary, and Red-billed Leiothrix. Ground-dwellers include large coveys of California Quail, flocks of Wild Turkey, and solitary Erckel's Francolins and Common Pheasants.

11. Hakalau Forest National Wildlife Refuge, Hawai'i. This was the first national wildlife refuge established solely for the benefit of forest birds. Although it is the best place on the Big Island to see a variety of native birds, it is remote and visits require considerable advance planning and expense. The refuge is open to the general public only on certain weekends, and the access road requires a four-wheel-drive vehicle. Another way to visit the refuge is with a professional guide. Rob Pacheco of Hawai'i Forest & Trail (Box 2975, Kailua-Kona HI 96745; 808/329-1993) conducts regular tours of this and other areas. Logistics aside, the refuge is a delightful place with good populations of Hawaiian Hawk, 'Akepa, Hawai'i Creeper, and 'Akiapola'au along with the more common 'I'iwi, 'Apapane, Hawai'i 'Amakihi, 'Oma'o, and Hawai'i 'Elepaio. In the ranch lands along the road into the refuge, game birds such as Erckel's Francolin, Chukar, Wild Turkey, and California Quail may

be seen, and stock ponds may have breeding pairs of Hawaiian Duck or wintering waterfowl. These montane pastures are surprisingly a major staging area for Pacific Golden-Plovers and Ruddy Turnstones before they head north in the spring, and Eurasian Skylarks are abundant. For the most recent information write Refuge Manager, Hakalau Forest National Wildlife Refuge, 154 Waianuenue Ave., Rm. 219, Hilo HI 96720, or phone (808) 933-6915.

12. Hawai'i Volcanoes National Park, Hawai'i. Although its most famous feature is Kilauea Volcano, this national park also preserves some excellent habitats for birds. In and around Kilauea Caldera, the heart of the park, 'Apapane seem as common as the ubiquitous Japanese White-eyes and the loud songs of 'Oma'o enliven the forests. One can also find Chukar, White-tailed Tropicbird, Nene, and Hawaiian Hawk. The entrance to Thurston Lava Tube is probably the best place to get a look at the hard-to-see 'Oma'o, as well as Hawai'i 'Amakihi and Hawai'i 'Elepaio. A drive down spectacular ain of Craters Road takes one to the coastal cliffs where Black Noddies nest. e main portion of the park charges an entrance fee, but the area called the una Loa Strip is open without charge via Mauna Loa Road off Highway 11 st of the main park entrance. Kipuka Puaulu is also known as Bird Park, but ding is actually better further up the road in Kipuka Ki. Both harbor

Hawai'i 'Elepaio, 'Oma'o, Hawaiian Hawk, Hawai'i 'Amakihi, Red-billed Leiothrix, Melodious Laughing-thrush, and Kalij Pheasant. Late in the day, the pheasants and California Quail often sit on the road itself. The 'ohi'a and koa trees at the upper end of the road are the best place in the park to find 'I'iwi. For information, write The Superintendent, Hawai'i Volcanoes National Park, Box 52, Hawai'i National Park HI 96718, or call (808) 967-7311.

FOR FURTHER INFORMATION

This book introduced you to Hawai'i's beautiful and interesting avifauna. We hope you will want to learn more, and the following references will help.

BERGER, ANDREW J. 1981. *Hawaiian Birdlife.* 2nd. Ed. Univ. of Hawai'i Press, Honolulu. (The standard home reference "state bird book." Includes quotations from much older literature that make fascinating reading.)

HARRISON, CRAIG S. 1990. *Seabirds of Hawai'i: Natural History and Conservation.* Cornell Univ. Press, Ithaca and London.

HAWAI'I AUDUBON SOCIETY. 1993. *Hawaii's Birds.* 4th. Ed. Honolulu: Hawai'i Audubon Society. (Widely available in Hawai'i or by mail from the Society at P. O. Box 22832, Honolulu HI 96822. A useful first field guide illustrated with photographs.)

PRATT, H. DOUGLAS. 1996a. *Enjoying Birds in Hawai'i: A Birdfinding Guide to the Fiftieth State.* 2nd. Edition. Mutual Publishing, Honolulu. (Gives detailed directions to 50 birding sites, plus details for finding virtually all of Hawai'i's rare birds. Available from the Society at the above address.)

PRATT, H. DOUGLAS. 1996b. *Voices of Hawaii's Birds: An Audio Companion to Hawaii's Birds.* (Two cassettes designed to be used with *Hawaii's Birds*, but also useful without it. Includes recordings of nearly all species found in Hawai'i today.)

PRATT, H. DOUGLAS, PHILLIP L. BRUNER, and DELWYN G. BERRETT. 1987. *A Field Guide to the Birds of Hawai'i and the Tropical Pacific.* Princeton, N. J.: Princeton Univ. Press. (This is the only field guide to list and illustrate all birds in Hawai'i. Also includes birds of Micronesia and Polynesia.)

PYLE, ROBERT L. 1988. Checklist of the Birds of Hawai'i - 1988. *'Elepaio* 48: 95-106. (The "official" state checklist. Available for $2.00 from the Hawaii Audubon Society at the above address.)

ABOUT THE AUTHOR

■

Dr. H. Douglas Pratt is an ornithologist, illustrator, and ecotour leader who has been studying Hawaiian birds since 1974. He is senior author and illustrator of the definitive *A Field Guide to the Birds of Hawaii and the Tropical Pacific* (Princeton University Press). His Hawai'i works include our popular birdfinding guide *Enjoying Birds in Hawaii* and *Hawai'i's Beautiful Birds*, as well as the Hawaii Audubon *Society's Voices of Hawaii's Birds*, a 2-cassette guide to bird sounds. His scientific writings have been published in many scientific journals and his paintings and photographs have appeared in such well-known publications as *Audubon, National Wildlife, National Geographic, Defenders,* and *Encyclopaedia Britannica.* Dr. Pratt lives in Baton Rouge, Louisiana, where he is a Staff Research Associate of the Louisiana State University Museum of Natural Science. He travels frequently to Hawai'i to lead nature tours and conduct scientific research.

ABOUT THE PHOTOGRAPHER

■

Jack Jeffrey of Hilo is the most capable wildlife photographer working in Hawai'i today. As a biologist with the National Biological Service, he is intimately familiar with the isolated strongholds of Hawai'i's remaining native birds and has taken pictures of many species that defied the best efforts of previous photographers. He combines a naturalist's curiosity with the patience and technical skill of a world-class photographer. The impressive list of publications that have featured his work includes *National Geographic, Audubon, Life, National Wildlife, Birder's World, Pacific Discovery,* and *Defenders.*

INDEX